SCHOLAST

Just-Right Glyphs
for Young Learners

by Pamela Chanko

New York · Toronto · London · Auckland · Sydney
Mexico City · New Delhi · Hong Kong · Buenos Aires

Teaching *Resources*

Edited by Immacula A. Rhodes

Cover design by Jason Robinson

Interior design by Sydney Wright

Cover illustrations by Rusty Fletcher and Sydney Wright

Interior illustrations by Maxie Chambliss, Rusty Fletcher, Karen Sevaly, and Sydney Wright

ISBN–13: 978-0-545-10292-6

ISBN–10: 0-545-10292-8

1 2 3 4 5 6 7 8 9 10   40   16 15 14 13 12 11 10

Contents

Introduction

They say that "a picture paints a thousand words," and nothing could be truer of that adage than a glyph! Glyphs (short for hieroglyphics) are pictures that convey information using visual attributes, and their capacity to teach mathematics, communication, and even early reading and writing skills is truly immense. How can a glyph activity accomplish so much? The key lies in its use of symbols. Learning to use and interpret symbols is a vital skill for every young child at school, because it is essential to nearly every curricular area. Letters are symbols that represent sounds. Words are symbols that represent ideas. Numbers are symbols that represent quantities and concepts. Symbols are what we use to represent abstract thought in a concrete, recognizable way.

Glyphs are particularly beneficial for building math skills because they focus on representing and analyzing data and statistics. This may sound quite advanced for kindergarten and first-grade students, but *Just-Right Glyphs for Young Learners* makes it easy! For example, children who use the sun-shaped eraser on their Back-to-School Pencil glyph are showing that painting is their favorite school activity, while children who use the apple-shaped eraser are communicating that they prefer block building. Those children are representing data. When children count and compare the number of red and orange pencils, they can learn which mode of travel—bus or car—is used most by children to get to school. They're analyzing statistics!

In kindergarten and first grade, children experience an onslaught of new information and ideas, so helping them make connections between those ideas is especially important. And that's exactly what the activities in this book are designed to help you do. The lessons are based on concepts and themes you already teach around the year, from weather to animals to plants to holidays. Creating the glyphs not only fits seamlessly into your curriculum, but also helps kids connect each topic to their own experiences, making it more meaningful to them. And all the while, they build math, vocabulary, and even social skills as they discover ways in which they are alike and different. Perhaps most important of all, making and using the glyphs is fun. As learning requirements become more complex and demanding, many teachers find themselves wondering where the fun of early childhood fits in. The key lies in teaching sophisticated skills in an engaging and enjoyable way—and you're holding it right in your hands!

How to Use This Book

The activities in this book are designed with the busy teacher in mind: all you need is a copier and a few classroom materials. The glyphs are presented season by season, beginning with fall, but you can do the activities in any order, or pick and choose those particularly relevant to your curriculum. (For instance, you'll find a ladybug glyph in the summer section, but you might use it during an insect theme in spring.) You'll also find an Anytime section with glyphs appropriate for any time of year. Each activity contains the following elements:

Sample Glyph: At the top of each lesson page, you'll find an illustration of a completed glyph. Call-outs point to each attribute and explain its meaning, giving you a feel for the whole activity at a glance.

Math Skills: Here, you'll find a list of key math skills addressed by the glyph and extension activities for easy reference.

Materials: Use this section to find out what you'll need to complete the glyph. In addition to the reproducible patterns, the glyphs generally use common classroom materials such as scissors, glue, crayons, and construction paper.

Getting Started: This section offers suggestions on how to prepare for the activity and introduce the glyph to children.

Creating the Glyph: Look here to find step-by-step instructions that help you guide children through the activity. For your reference, a detailed model lesson, which includes an example of dialogue with children, is provided on page 6. You might find the model especially helpful to review before you have children do their first glyph.

Extend Learning: The ideas in this section provide ways you can help children use their completed glyphs to analyze data and build critical thinking skills. Activities let you reinforce a variety of skills, including sorting, graphing, ordering, comparing and contrasting, using the process of elimination, and drawing logical conclusions.

Tip: Some activities include a tip that suggests an additional way to use the glyph.

Legend: This page serves as both the student directions and the key for completing the glyph activity. Here, you'll find several questions for children to respond to along with answers that they choose from. Illustrations are provided to help support children's understanding as they make their choices. You can display the completed glyphs along with a copy of the legend to serve as a reference as children interpret the meaning of each attribute.

Reproducible Patterns: Give children copies of these cut-and-paste patterns to use when creating their glyphs.

A Model Lesson

Use this sample lesson for Birthday Wishes as a guide for introducing the glyph.

STEP 1: In advance, complete your own Birthday Wishes glyph. Display the glyph and a copy of the legend to introduce it to children. Your introductory dialogue might begin as follows.

Sample Dialogue

Teacher: What can you tell me about this cupcake?
Student: There's a candle on it.
Student: It has pink icing and chocolate chips.
Teacher: Yes. This is a special cupcake I made about myself. The icing, candle, and chocolate chips tell things about me. I answered questions on the legend to make my cupcake. The legend tells what the different parts of the cupcake mean. For example, the first question asks "In what month is your birthday?" I answered the question, then colored the icing on my cupcake based on the color assigned to that month. The four choices are light blue, pink, light green, and yellow. What color is the icing on my cupcake?
Student: Pink.
Teacher: So what does that tell you about my birthday? In what month is it?

Student: It's in April, May, or June!
Teacher: Yes! My birthday is in May.
Student: My birthday is in January.
Teacher: So what color would you make your icing?
Student: I would like to make mine pink, too.
Teacher: Why?
Student: Because it's my favorite!
Teacher: Pink icing is yummy. But remember, this cupcake is special. The color of the icing tells when your birthday is. Let's look at the legend again. It says to color the icing light blue if your birthday is in January. So what color would your icing be?
Student: Light blue!
Teacher: Yes! That way, when people see your cupcake, they will know your birthday is in January, February, or March.

Continue, following a similar procedure to introduce the other attributes of your glyph: the type of the candle that shows your age range, and the shape of the candy toppings, which shows what you would most enjoy about a birthday party.

STEP 2: Give children a copy of the glyph legend and patterns. Then guide them through the steps to create their glyph. Read each question aloud and give children time to complete the step before continuing. As children work, circulate around the room and comment on the attributes they choose, reminding them what each means.

STEP 3: Display the completed glyphs and discuss their attributes, using a dialogue similar to the one in Step 1. Encourage children to compare and contrast their cupcakes, helping them use the data to answer questions. For example, you might say: *How many children have a birthday in October, November, or December? Count the cupcakes with yellow icing to find out!* Or say: *What do most children say they would enjoy most about a birthday party? Use the candy toppings on the cupcakes to figure out the answer.* After guiding children to answer general questions about their glyphs, you might have them do the extension activity—in this case, working together to create a birthday timeline with their glyphs.

Modifying and Leveling the Glyphs

Teachers often find themselves faced with a dilemma when choosing ready-to-use lessons and materials. On the one hand, the convenience is unparalleled—there's no need to prepare your own drawings or text! On the other hand, the materials might not be at exactly the right level for all students, or they might need tweaking to better fit your curriculum needs. That's where the power of flexibility comes in—and with *Just-Right Glyphs for Young Learners*, you've got it! Each activity is ready-to-go, but can also be easily tailored to meet your students' needs using these quick tips.

Adding More Features: You can increase the number of attributes for any glyph by adding more questions to the legend. You might expand the legend to make the glyph more challenging for advanced students or to extend the topic covered by a particular glyph. Simply write the additional questions and attributes used to represent them, along with the answer choices, on the back of the legend page, on a separate sheet, or on chart paper. For example, for Frosty the Snow-Glyph, you might add the question "How would you most like to warm up on a cold day?" and have children color the hat according to their answer. The answer choices might include: "sit by a fireplace" (*red*); "drink hot cocoa" (*blue*); and "eat soup" (*green*). To answer another question, you might have children add designs to the mittens or gloves. You can also add more answer choices to an existing question on the legend by giving children an additional color or pattern option.

Simplifying the Glyphs: To make a glyph easier for lower level students, or to simply create a "quickie" activity, you can easily remove an option from any glyph. For instance, you might remove a question from Cornucopia of Thanks by cutting or crossing out a question on the legend and not distributing the corresponding pattern (such as the corn or pumpkin patterns). Another method of simplification is to remove an answer choice from one or more questions, or to pre-assemble part of the glyph before having children complete it. (For example, for Summer Sandcastle, you might assemble the sandcastle using one tower type and then remove the first question and tower options from the legend.)

Customizing the Glyphs: If you have a special question you'd like to ask students, just use correction fluid or tape to mask an existing question and responses on the legend, then replace them with the new text. For example, in the Back-to-School Pencil activity, if you would rather have children indicate their choice of snack rather than the kind of character they'd like to read about, simply mask that question and replace it with "What would you most like to eat at snack time?" Then replace the two answer options with two snack options, such as "graham crackers" and "pretzels." Copy a class set, and you've got a customized glyph in a snap!

Connections to the
NCTM Standards

The activities in this book correspond to the standards recommended by the National Council of Teachers of Mathematics (NCTM).

Glyph Activity	Content Standards					Process Standards			
	Numbers and Operations	Algebra	Geometry	Measurement	Data Analysis and Probability	Problem Solving	Reasoning and Proof	Communication	Connections
Back-to-School Pencil	●		●		●	●	●	●	●
Apple-Picking Time	●	●			●	●	●	●	●
Cornucopia of Thanks	●	●	●		●	●	●	●	●
Frosty the Snow-Glyph	●	●		●	●	●	●	●	●
Happy Holidays		●	●		●	●	●	●	●
Sweet Valentine	●	●	●		●	●	●	●	●
Ready for Rain		●	●		●	●	●	●	●
Look Who's Hatching!		●	●		●	●	●	●	●
Build-a-Bloom	●		●		●	●	●	●	●
I Spot a Ladybug!	●	●	●		●	●	●	●	●
Summer Sandcastle	●		●		●	●	●	●	●
Let Freedom Ring	●	●	●		●	●	●	●	●
All-About-Me Hat	●	●	●		●	●	●	●	●
Birthday Wishes	●	●	●	●	●	●	●	●	●
Use Your Noodle!	●	●	●		●	●	●	●	●

National Council of Teachers of Mathematics. (2000). *Principles and Standards for School Mathematics.* Reston, VA: NCTM. www.nctm.org

Back-to-School Pencil

Whether children are returning from summer break or starting school for the first time, the beginning of the school year is always an exciting time. This glyph helps children share their favorite parts of school—and helps you get to know them better!

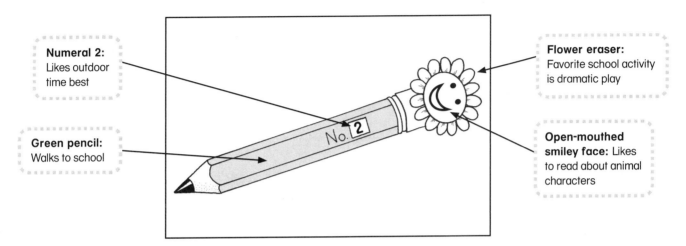

Numeral 2: Likes outdoor time best

Green pencil: Walks to school

No. 2

Flower eraser: Favorite school activity is dramatic play

Open-mouthed smiley face: Likes to read about animal characters

Getting Started

Create your own glyph and mark your responses on the legend. Then display your glyph and discuss it with children. Guide them to use the legend to determine what each feature on the glyph tells about you.

Creating the Glyph

1. Cut out the pencil and glue it to construction paper. Leave room for the eraser at the top.

2. Read and answer each question on the legend. Follow these directions to represent your answers on the glyph:
- Question 1: Color the pencil.
- Question 2: Write the numeral in the box on the pencil.
- Question 3: Cut out the eraser that corresponds to your answer. Glue it to the top of the pencil.
- Question 4: Draw a face on the eraser.

3. Color the eraser. Write your name on the back of the glyph.

Extend Learning

Use the glyphs to decide which book to read at story time! First, choose two books: one with human characters and the other with animal characters. Next, have children sort the glyphs by the type of smiley face and count the glyphs in each group. Then help them determine which book is represented by the group with the most glyphs. Finally, read that book aloud to the class.

Math Skills

❋ number recognition
❋ geometry: shapes
❋ counting
❋ comparing quantities

Materials

❋ glyph legend and patterns (pages 10–11)
❋ 9- by 12-inch construction paper
❋ scissors
❋ glue
❋ crayons

Name_____

Back-to-School Pencil
Legend

1 **How do you get to school?**

	bus	car	walk	another way
Color of Pencil	**red**	**orange**	**green**	**yellow**

2 **What part of the school day do you like best?**

	circle time	outdoor time	snack time
Numeral in Box	**1**	**2**	**3**

3 **What is your favorite school activity?**

	painting	block building	dramatic play	another activity
Shape of Eraser				

4 **What kind of characters do you most like to read about at story time?**

	human characters	animal characters
Face on Eraser	:)	:D

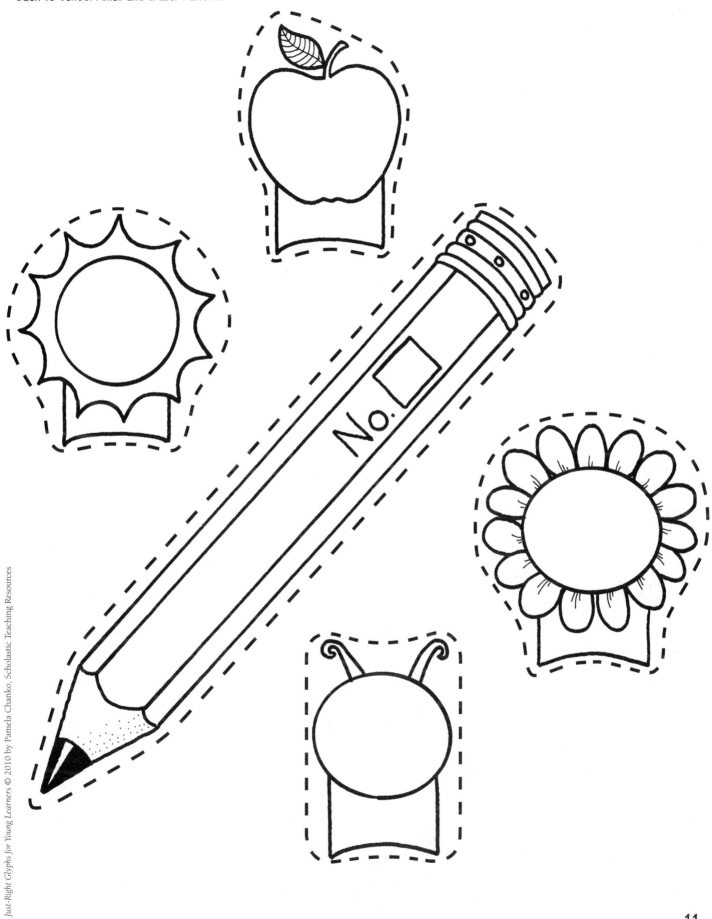

Apple-Picking Time

Celebrate the autumn harvest with an imaginary trip to the apple orchard!
Red, green, and yellow apples are all juicy and ripe for the picking.
This glyph helps children share and compare their experiences with apples.

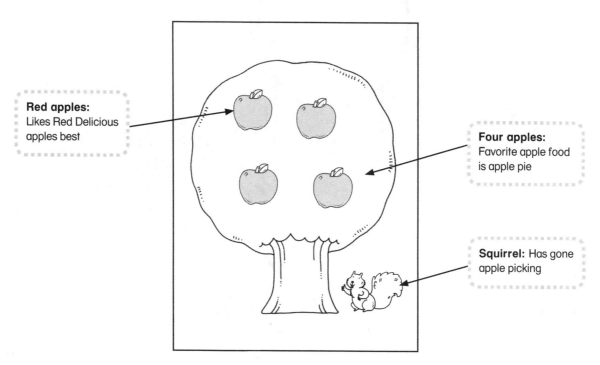

Red apples: Likes Red Delicious apples best

Four apples: Favorite apple food is apple pie

Squirrel: Has gone apple picking

Getting Started

Create your own glyph and mark your responses on the legend. Then display your glyph and discuss it with children. Guide them to use the legend to determine what each feature on the glyph tells about your experiences with apples.

Creating the Glyph

1. Color and cut out the apple tree. Glue it to construction paper.

2. Read and answer each question on the legend. Follow these directions to represent your answers on the glyph:
- Question 1: Cut out the number of apples that corresponds to your answer.
- Question 2: Color your apples. Glue them to the tree.
- Question 3: Color and cut out the animal that corresponds to your answer. Glue it next to the tree trunk.

3. Write your name on the back of the glyph.

Extend Learning

Choose one "secret" attribute by which to sort the glyphs, such as the color of apples on the tree. Arrange the glyphs into groups and invite children to guess the sorting rule. Then repeat, using a different sorting rule (such as number of apples).

Math Skills
- counting
- positional concepts

Materials
- glyph legend and patterns (pages 13–15)
- 9- by 12-inch construction paper
- crayons
- scissors
- glue

Name _____

1 **What is your favorite apple food?**

	apple juice	applesauce	apple pie
Number of Apples			

2 **What kind of apple do you like best?**

	Red Delicious	Granny Smith	Golden Delicious
Color of Apples	**red**	**green**	**yellow**

3 **Have you ever gone apple picking?**

	yes	no
Animal Next to Tree		

Just-Right Glyphs for Young Learners © 2010 by Pamela Chanko, Scholastic Teaching Resources

13

Cornucopia of Thanks

The harvest is in, and it's time to celebrate! Encourage children to share
about themselves on Thanksgiving—from favorite foods to things they feel thankful for.
As children fill these cornucopias, they will also be filling the classroom with data!

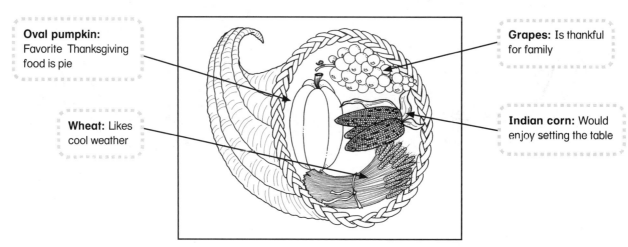

Oval pumpkin: Favorite Thanksgiving food is pie

Wheat: Likes cool weather

Grapes: Is thankful for family

Indian corn: Would enjoy setting the table

Getting Started

Create your own glyph and mark your responses on the legend. Then display your
glyph and discuss it with children. Guide them to use the legend to determine the
meaning of each feature on the glyph.

Creating the Glyph

1. Color and cut out the cornucopia. Glue it to a horizontal sheet of construction paper.

2. Read and answer Questions 1–4 on the legend. Color and cut out the item that
corresponds to your answer for each question.

3. Glue the four items to the opening of the cornucopia. The items may overlap slightly
or extend beyond the opening of the cornucopia.

4. Write your name on the back of the glyph.

Extend Learning

Help children sort out the glyphs that have at least two attributes in common (such as a
pear-shaped pumpkin and two ears of un-shucked corn). Ask them to find any glyphs
within those groups that share an additional feature (such as grapes). Then have them
look for a fourth common attribute among the glyphs. Are there two or more glyphs
that share all four attributes? If so, turn over the glyphs to find out which children these
"perfect" matches belong to!

TIP Use the glyph as a springboard to discuss food groups and nutrition.

Math Skills

* geometry: shapes
* positional concepts
* counting

Materials

* glyph legend and patterns (pages 17–20)
* 9- by 12-inch construction paper in fall colors
* crayons
* scissors
* glue

Name _____

Cornucopia of Thanks
Legend

1 **What are you most thankful for on Thanksgiving?**

	food	friends	family
Fruit			

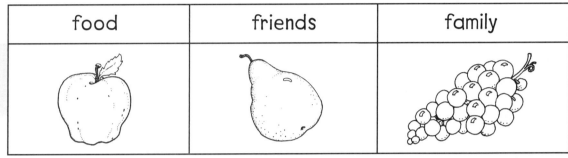

2 **What is your favorite Thanksgiving food?**

	turkey	stuffing	pie	a different food
Pumpkin Shape				

3 **What Thanksgiving job would you most enjoy doing?**

	shopping for food	setting the table	washing the dishes
Type of Corn			

4 **What do you like most about fall?**

	cool weather	colorful leaves	beginning of school
Nature Item			

Just-Right Glyphs for Young Learners © 2010 by Pamela Chanko, Scholastic Teaching Resources

Cornucopia of Thanks
Fruit and Pumpkin Patterns

Just-Right Glyphs for Young Learners © 2010 by Pamela Chanko, Scholastic Teaching Resources

❊ ❊ Frosty the Snow-Glyph ❊ ❊

Playing in the snow makes wintertime well worth the cold temperatures—
and what could be more fun than building a person made of snow?
With this glyph, children share how they feel about frosty weather.

Pom-pom hat: Favorite thing to make with snow is snowballs

Broom: Would like to get more snow

Striped scarf: Favorite winter sport is ice-skating

Mittens: Likes snow a lot

Getting Started

Create your own glyph and mark your responses on the legend. Then display your glyph and discuss it with children. Guide them to use the legend to determine what each feature on the glyph tells about your wintertime preferences.

Creating the Glyph

1. Cut out the snow person. Glue it to a vertical sheet of construction paper.

2. Read and answer each question on the legend. Follow these directions to represent your answers on the glyph:
   • Questions 1–3: Color and cut out the item that corresponds to your answer for each question. Glue the items onto the snow person.
   • Question 4: Color and cut out the snow tool that corresponds to your answer. Glue it to one of the snow person's hands.

3. Color and add extra details to the snow person, if desired. (Avoid covering up any designs or patterns that show data.) Write your name on the back of the glyph.

Extend Learning

Invite children to guess which winter sport is the class favorite. Then ask: *How can you use the glyphs to find the answer?* One method children might use is to sort the glyphs by the pattern on the scarves, count the number in each group to see which has the most, then check the legend to discover which sport that scarf pattern stands for.

Math Skills

❊ positional concepts
❊ patterns
❊ counting

Materials

❊ glyph legends and patterns (pages 22–25)
❊ 9- by 12-inch construction paper in dark colors
❊ scissors
❊ glue
❊ crayons

TIP Use the glyph as a springboard to discuss ways to stay safe and warm in winter weather.

Name _____

Frosty the Snow-Glyph
❄ Legend ❄

1 **How much do you like snow?**

	a lot	a little
Hand Covering		

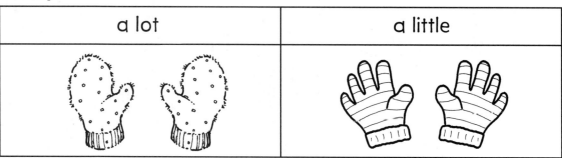

2 **What is your favorite thing to make with snow?**

	snow person	snowballs	snow fort
Type of Hat			

3 **What winter sport do you like most?**

	sledding	ice-skating	skiing
Scarf Design			

4 **Would you like to get more snow where you live?**

	yes	no
Snow Tool		

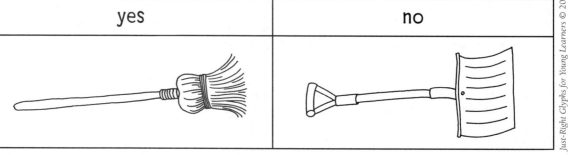

Just-Right Glyphs for Young Learners © 2010 by Pamela Chanko, Scholastic Teaching Resources

Frosty the Snow-Glyph

Hat, Hand Covering, and Scarf Patterns

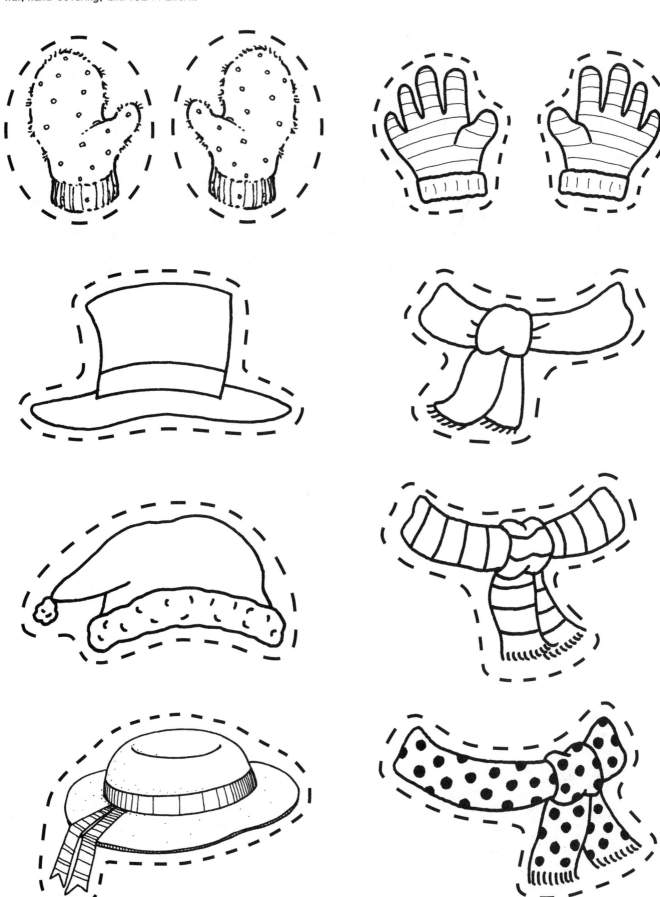

Just-Right Glyphs for Young Learners © 2010 by Pamela Chanko, Scholastic Teaching Resources

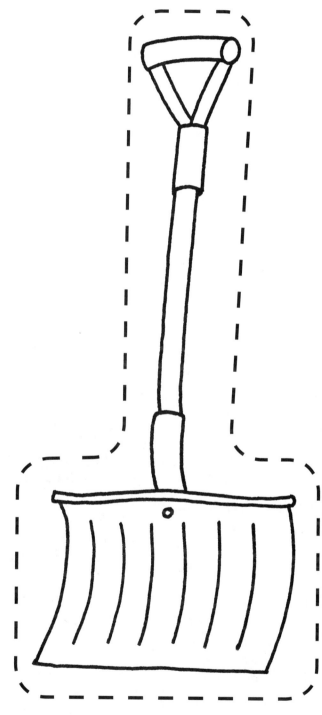

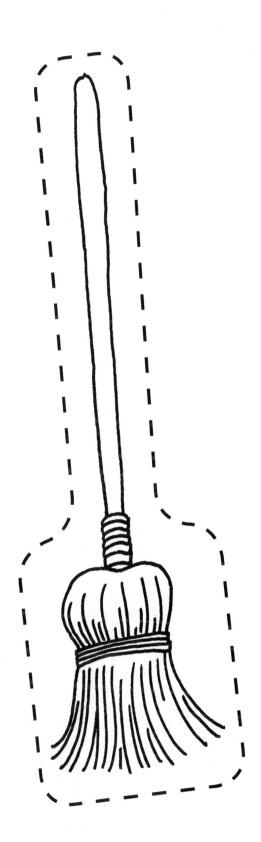

Just-Right Glyphs for Young Learners © 2010 by Pamela Chanko, Scholastic Teaching Resources

Happy Holidays

Nothing brightens up the winter like the holidays! While celebrations
may differ, the spirit of holiday cheer helps bring people together.
With this glyph, children share what makes the season special to them.

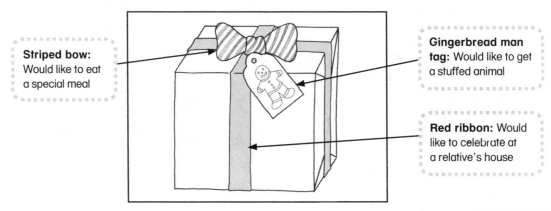

Striped bow:
Would like to eat
a special meal

**Gingerbread man
tag:** Would like to get
a stuffed animal

Red ribbon: Would
like to celebrate at
a relative's house

Getting Started

Create your own glyph and mark your responses on the legend. Then display your glyph
and discuss it with children. Guide them to use the legend to determine what each feature
on the glyph tells about your favorite ways to celebrate the holidays.

Creating the Glyph

1. Cut out the gift. Glue it to a sheet of construction paper.

2. Read and answer each question on the legend. Follow these directions to
represent your answers on the glyph:
- Question 1: Find the color that corresponds to your answer. Color the ribbon
  on the gift that color.
- Questions 2–3: Color and cut out the bow and tag that correspond to your
  answer for each question. Glue them to the gift.

3. Draw designs on the gift to create decorative "gift wrap," if desired. (Avoid covering up the
ribbon color or any patterns that show data.) Write your name on the back of the glyph.

Extend Learning

Invite children to sort the glyphs by ribbon color. Point to the group with a blue ribbon
and ask: *What do the creators of these glyphs have in common?* (They would like to celebrate
the holidays at home.) Then have children sort this group by another attribute—such as
shape of bow—and identify the additional shared characteristic (such as *likes to sing songs*).
Continue creating groups and subgroups with the glyphs to help children discover their
shared holiday preferences.

TIP Use the glyph as a springboard to discuss winter holidays
around the world.

Math Skills

- ❖ geometry: shapes
- ❖ positional concept

Materials

- ❖ glyph legend
  and patterns
  (pages 27–29)
- ❖ 9- by 12-inch
  construction paper
- ❖ scissors
- ❖ glue
- ❖ crayons

Name _____

Happy Holidays
Legend

1 **Where would you most like to celebrate the winter holidays?**

	at home	at a relative's house	at a friend's house	somewhere else
Ribbon Color	**blue**	**red**	**green**	**yellow**

2 **What holiday tradition would you most like to do?**

	decorate	sing songs	eat a special meal	something else
Shape of Bow				

3 **What kind of holiday gift would you most like to get?**

	stuffed animal	toy or game	sports gear	something else
Design on Tag				

Just-Right Glyphs for Young Learners © 2010 by Pamela Chanko, Scholastic Teaching Resources

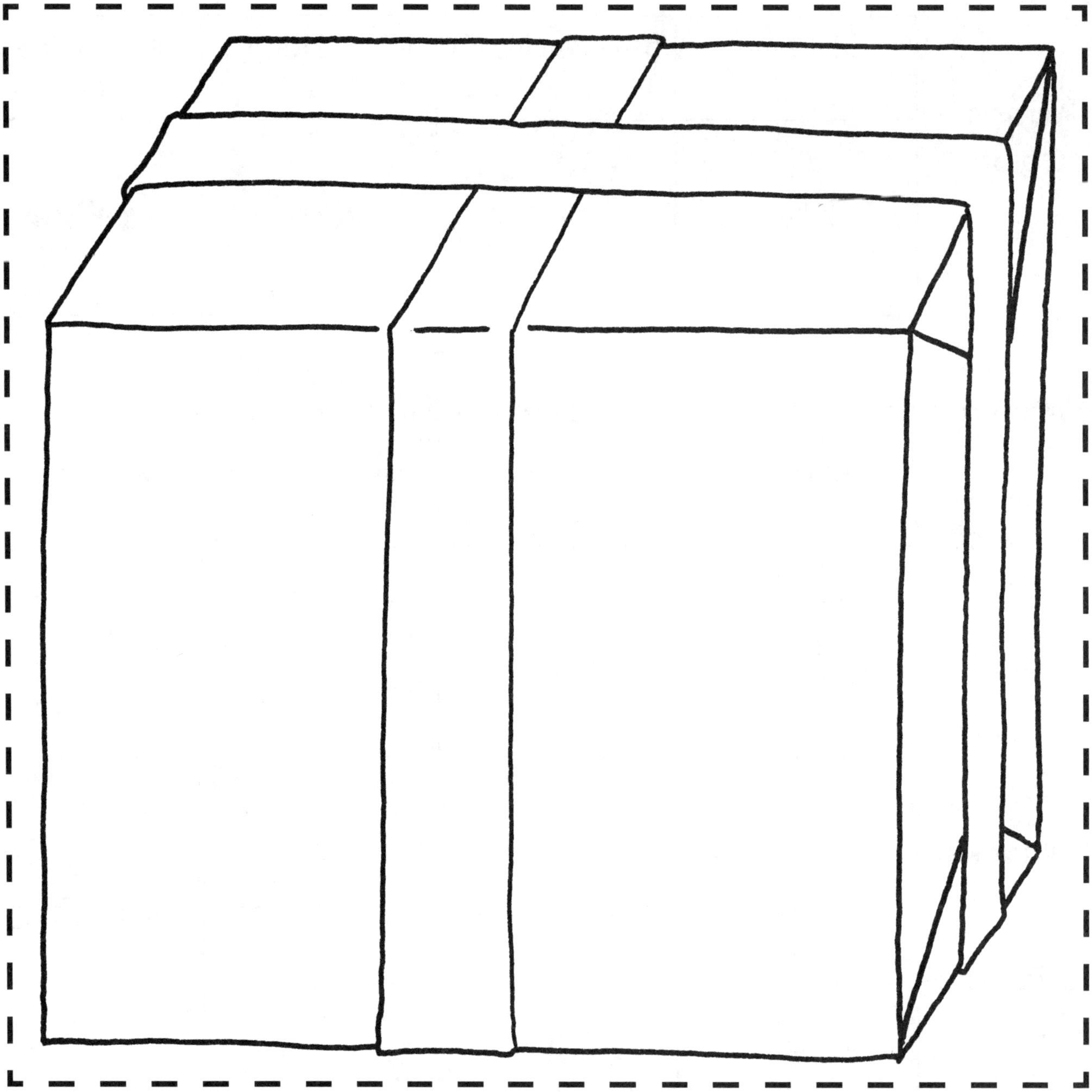

❄ ❄ Sweet Valentine ❄ ❄

Designing a box of candy can be just as much fun as receiving one!
This glyph helps children celebrate Valentine's Day by focusing on meaningful aspects
of the holiday: showing love to others and taking care of their heart!

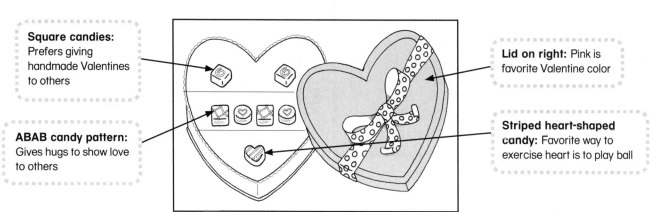

Square candies: Prefers giving handmade Valentines to others

ABAB candy pattern: Gives hugs to show love to others

Lid on right: Pink is favorite Valentine color

Striped heart-shaped candy: Favorite way to exercise heart is to play ball

Getting Started

Create your own glyph and mark your responses on the legend. Then display your glyph and discuss it with children. Guide them to use the legend to determine what each feature on the glyph tells about your Valentine-related preferences.

Creating the Glyph

1. Cut out the candy box. Glue it to a horizontal sheet of construction paper.

2. Read and answer each question on the legend. Follow these directions to represent your answers on the glyph:
  • Question 1: Glue the lid to the side of the candy box according to your answer.
  • Questions 2–3: Color and cut out the candy patterns that correspond to your answer for each question. Glue them to the candy box where indicated. Note that Question 1 focuses on the candy shape, Question 2 focuses on the pattern sequence of the candy, and Question 3 focuses on the design on the candy.

3. Color the glyph. (Avoid covering up any designs that show data.) Write your name on the back of the glyph.

Extend Learning

To give practice in the process of elimination, display the glyphs and secretly choose one for children to guess. Then give a single clue about that glyph, for instance: *My secret glyph has a pink bow.* Invite a volunteer to remove all the glyphs that do not have that attribute. Repeat, providing one clue at a time until only one glyph is left—the secret glyph!

TIP Use the glyph as a springboard to discuss the heart and how to keep it healthy.

Math Skills

❖ positional concepts
❖ geometry: shapes
❖ patterns

Materials

❖ glyph legend and patterns (pages 31–33)
❖ 12- by 18-inch construction paper
❖ scissors
❖ glue
❖ crayons

Name _____

Sweet Valentine
❄ Legend ❄

1 **What is your favorite Valentine color?**

	red	pink
Position of Lid	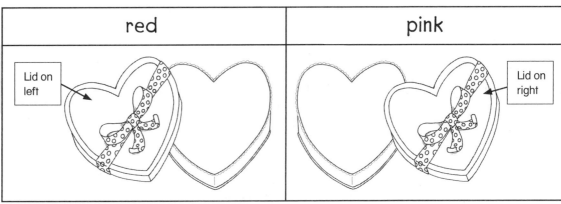	

2 **What kind of Valentines would you prefer to give to others?**

	handmade Valentines	store-bought Valentines
Candy Shape	(candy) (candy)	(candy) (candy)

3 **How do you like to show others that you love them?**

	give hugs	draw picture	be helpful	say "I Love You"
Candy Pattern				

4 **What is your favorite way to exercise your heart?**

	run	ride a bike or trike	play ball
Design on Heart Candy	(heart candy)	(heart candy)	(heart candy)

Just-Right Glyphs for Young Learners © 2010 by Pamela Chanko, Scholastic Teaching Resources

Sweet Valentine
Box and Candy Patterns

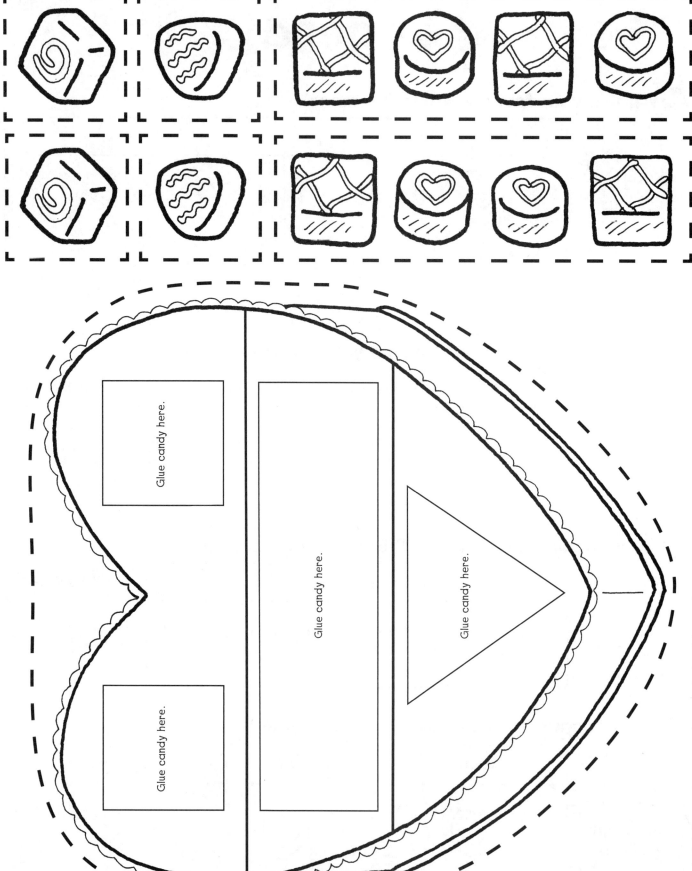

Just-Right Glyphs for Young Learners © 2010 by Pamela Chanko, Scholastic Teaching Resources

Sweet Valentine

Lid and Candy Patterns

Just-Right Glyphs for Young Learners © 2010 by Pamela Chanko, Scholastic Teaching Resources

Ready for Rain

Spring can be a wonderful, splishy-splashy time of year! Get children excited about spring weather by inviting them to design their own unique umbrella. Whether they prefer puddle-jumping or staying indoors, children will enjoy creating this rainy-day glyph.

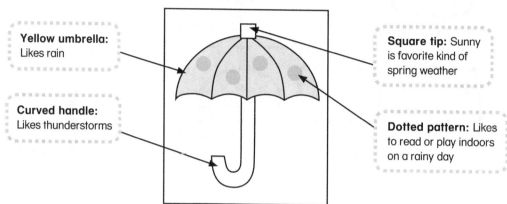

Yellow umbrella: Likes rain

Curved handle: Likes thunderstorms

Square tip: Sunny is favorite kind of spring weather

Dotted pattern: Likes to read or play indoors on a rainy day

Getting Started

Create your own glyph and mark your responses on the legend. Then display your glyph and discuss it with children. Guide them to use the legend to determine what each feature on the glyph tells about your rainy-day and spring weather preferences.

Creating the Glyph

1. Cut out the umbrella top. Glue it near the top of a vertical sheet of construction paper.

2. Read and answer each question on the legend. Follow these directions to represent your answers on the glyph:
- Question 1: Color the umbrella top.
- Question 2: Use a dark crayon to draw a pattern on the umbrella top.
- Questions 3–4: Cut out the handle and tip that corresponds to each answer. Glue each piece to the umbrella top.

3. Color the handle and tip. Write your name on the back of the glyph.

Extend Learning

Draw two overlapping circles to create a Venn Diagram. Label each circle with "Likes Rain" or "Likes Thunderstorms." Label the overlapping section with "Likes Both." Help children analyze their umbrella glyphs to determine which, if any, attributes from the diagram apply. Then have them place a sticky note labeled with their name on the appropriate section of the diagram. If their glyph does not fit any of the attributes, have them place their sticky note outside the diagram.

TIP Use the glyph as a springboard to discuss the water cycle.

Math Skills
* patterns
* geometry: shapes
* positional concepts

Materials
* glyph legend and patterns (pages 35–36)
* 9- by 12-inch construction paper
* scissors
* glue
* crayons

Name _____

Legend

❶ Do you like rain?

	yes	no
Color of Umbrella	**yellow**	**light blue**

❷ What do you most like to do on a rainy day?

	watch the rain	splash in puddles	read or play indoors
Pattern on Umbrella			

❸ How do you feel about thunderstorms?

	I like them	I don't like them
Type of Handle	J	❘

❹ What is your favorite kind of spring weather?

	rainy	windy	sunny	stormy
Shape of Umbrella Tip	○	♡	☐	△

Just-Right Glyphs for Young Learners © 2010 by Pamela Chanko, Scholastic Teaching Resources

Just-Right Glyphs for Young Learners © 2010 by Pamela Chanko, Scholastic Teaching Resources

Look Who's Hatching!

Spring has sprung, and new life is bursting out everywhere!
This adorable glyph helps children think about a baby chick's
development while making connections to their own.

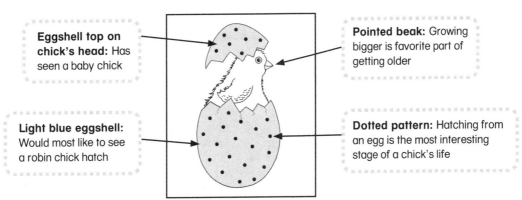

Eggshell top on chick's head: Has seen a baby chick

Pointed beak: Growing bigger is favorite part of getting older

Light blue eggshell: Would most like to see a robin chick hatch

Dotted pattern: Hatching from an egg is the most interesting stage of a chick's life

Getting Started

Create your own glyph and mark your responses on the legend. Then display your glyph and discuss it with children. Guide them to use the legend to determine what each feature on the glyph tells about you.

Creating the Glyph

1. Cut out the hatching chick pattern. Glue it to a vertical sheet of construction paper.

2. Read and answer each question on the legend. Follow these directions to represent your answers on the glyph:

- Question 1: Cut out the eggshell top. Glue it in the position that corresponds to your answer.
- Question 2: Color the top and bottom eggshells.
- Question 3: Use a dark crayon to draw a pattern on both parts of the eggshell.
- Question 4: Cut out the beak that corresponds to your answer. Glue it to the chick.

3. Color the chick and its beak. Write your name on the back of the glyph.

Extend Learning

Arrange several glyphs in a row, using one attribute to create a pattern. For instance, you might display the glyphs that have blue and green eggshells in an alternating color pattern (blue, green, blue, green). Challenge children to examine the glyphs to find the pattern. Then help children use the glyphs to create additional patterns, such as pointed beak, rounded beak, pointed beak, rounded beak. Encourage them to come up with a variety of patterns, such as AAB, AABB, and ABCABC.

TIP Use the glyph as a springboard to discuss the life cycle of a chick.

Math Skills

- ❋ positional concepts
- ❋ patterns
- ❋ geometry: shapes

Materials

- ❋ glyph legend and patterns (pages 38–39)
- ❋ 9- by 12-inch construction paper
- ❋ scissors
- ❋ glue
- ❋ crayons

Name _____

Look Who's Hatching!

Legend

1 **Have you ever seen a baby chick?**

	yes	no
Position of Eggshell Top		

2 **What kind of chick would you most like to see hatch?**

	chicken	duck	robin	another bird
Color of Eggshell	**light gray**	**light brown**	**light blue**	**light green**

3 **What stage of a chick's life is most interesting to you?**

	growing inside the egg	hatching from egg	learning to fly	growing into an adult
Pattern on Eggshell				

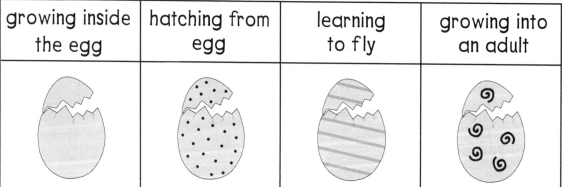

4 **What is your favorite part of getting older?**

	learning new things	growing bigger
Shape of Beak		

Just-Right Glyphs for Young Learners © 2010 by Pamela Chanko, Scholastic Teaching Resources

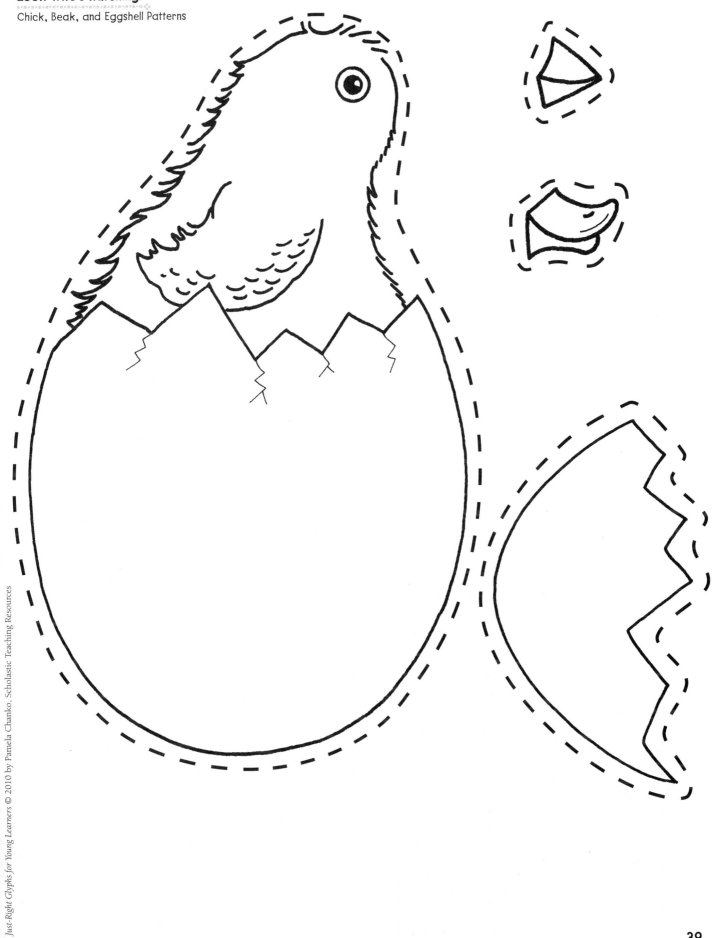

Build-a-Bloom

Plant the seeds of learning! Invite children to build their own bloom, petal by petal, as they share about gardening. The result will be a beautiful, data-filled flower—no green thumb required!

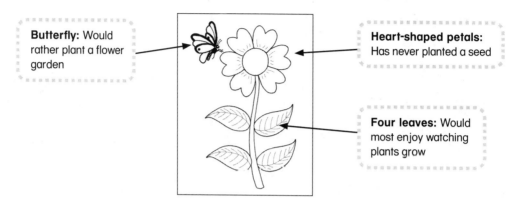

Butterfly: Would rather plant a flower garden

Heart-shaped petals: Has never planted a seed

Four leaves: Would most enjoy watching plants grow

Getting Started

Create your own glyph and mark your responses on the legend. Then display your glyph and discuss it with children. Guide them to use the legend to determine what each feature on the glyph tells about your gardening experiences and preferences.

Creating the Glyph

1. Color and cut out the stem pattern. Glue it to a vertical sheet of construction paper, placing the bottom of the stem near the bottom of the paper.

2. Read and answer each question on the legend. Follow these directions to represent your answers on the glyph:

- Question 1: Cut out the petals that correspond to your answer. Glue them around the circle at the top of the stem.
- Question 2: Cut out the number of leaves based on your answer. Glue them to the stem.
- Question 3: Cut out the insect that corresponds to your answer. Glue it near the flower.

3. Color the completed glyph. Then write your name on the back.

Extend Learning

Play a game of "Odd Man Out." First, display a group of glyphs that have something in common, such as the same petal shape. Also include one glyph that differs in that feature (a different petal shape). Then challenge children to identify the glyph that doesn't belong. After children become familiar with the game, invite them to create glyph groups and have classmates find the "odd man out."

TIP Use the glyph as a springboard to discuss plant needs and their growth.

Math Skills

❈ geometry: shapes
❈ counting
❈ comparing quantities

Materials

❈ glyph legend and patterns (pages 41–42)
❈ 9- by 12-inch construction paper
❈ crayons
❈ scissors
❈ glue

Name _____

Build-a-Bloom

Legend

1 **Have you ever planted a seed?**

yes	no
Petal Shape	

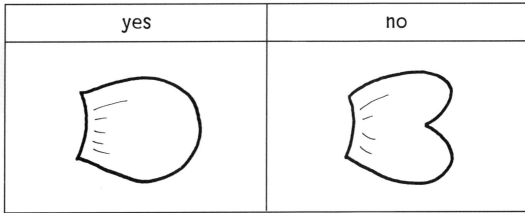

2 **What would you most enjoy about planting a garden?**

planting seeds	taking care of plants	watching plants grow

Number of Leaves

3 **Which kind of garden would you rather plant?**

a flower garden	a vegetable garden

Type of Insect

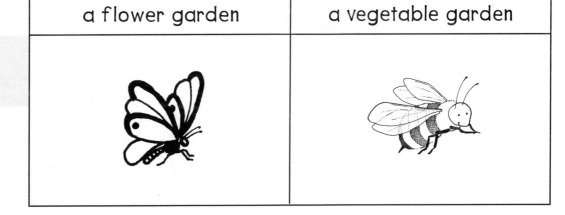

Just-Right Glyphs for Young Learners © 2010 by Pamela Chanko, Scholastic Teaching Resources

Build-a-Bloom
Flower and Insect Patterns

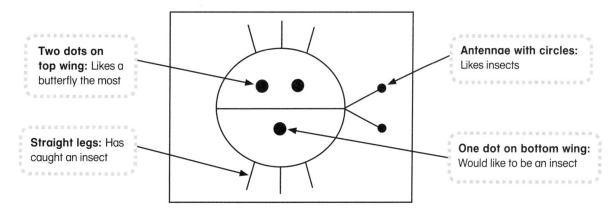

Two dots on top wing: Likes a butterfly the most

Straight legs: Has caught an insect

Antennae with circles: Likes insects

One dot on bottom wing: Would like to be an insect

Getting Started

Create your own glyph and mark your responses on the legend. Then display your glyph and discuss it with children. Guide them to use the legend to determine what each feature on the glyph tells about your insect-related experiences.

Creating the Glyph

1. Color the ladybug body red and cut it out. Glue it to the center of a horizontal sheet of construction paper, leaving room to draw legs and antennae.

2. Read and answer each question on the legend. Using a black crayon, follow these directions to represent your answers on the glyph:
- Questions 1–2: Draw the type of antennae and legs that corresponds to your answer for each question. Draw three legs on each side of the body.
- Questions 3–4: Draw the number of dots on the designated wing based on your answer to each question. Draw large dots.

3. Write your name on the back of the glyph.

Extend Learning

Display the glyphs and work with children to analyze the data. You might help them create a graph by sorting the glyphs into three vertical rows: ladybugs with one spot on the top wing, those with two spots on the top wing, and those with three spots on the top wing. Then have children use the graph and legend to determine which insect—ladybug, butterfly, or grasshopper—is the class favorite.

TIP Use the glyph as a springboard to discuss the characteristics of insects.

Math Skills

* geometry: shapes
* counting
* positional concepts

Materials

* glyph legend and patterns (pages 44–45)
* 12- by 18-inch construction paper in a light color
* scissors
* glue
* red and black crayons

Name _____

I Spot a Ladybug!

Legend

1 **Do you like insects?**

	yes	no
Type of Antennae	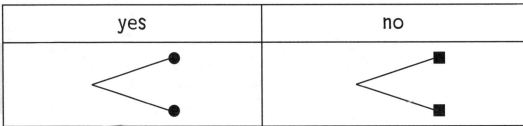	

2 **Have you ever caught an insect?**

	yes	no
Position of Legs	||	333

3 **What insect do you like most?**

	ladybug	butterfly	grasshopper
Dots on Top Wing	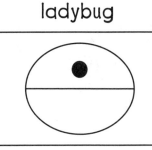		

4 **Would you like to be an insect?**

	yes	no
Dots on Bottom Wing	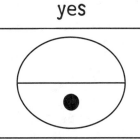	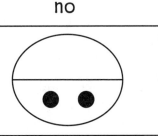

44

Just-Right Glyphs for Young Learners © 2010 by Pamela Chanko, Scholastic Teaching Resources

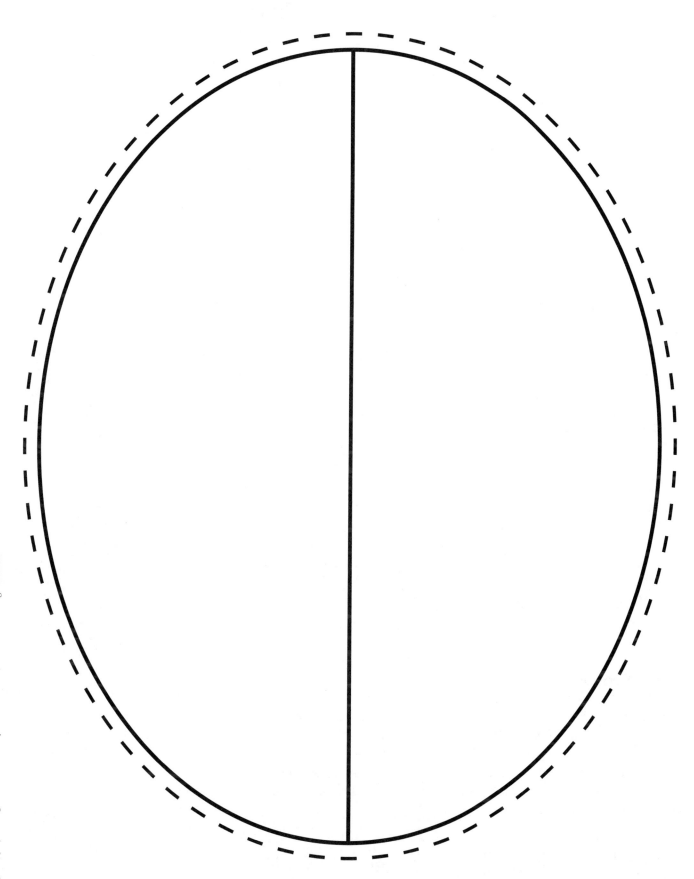

Summer Sandcastle

During those lazy, hazy days of summer, what could be better than a trip to the beach?
And a day at the beach is not complete without building a sandcastle! As children
design this sandcastle glyph, they'll provide data about their beach experiences!

Triangle flag: Would most enjoy swimming at the beach

Pointed towers: Has been to the beach

Clam shells: Would most like to have watermelon on a hot day

Yellow sandcastle: Has built a sandcastle

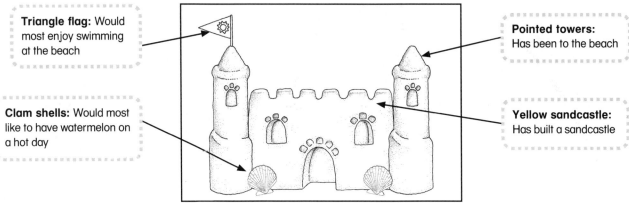

Getting Started

Create your own glyph and mark your responses on the legend. Then display your
glyph and discuss it with children. Guide them to use the legend to determine what
each feature on the glyph tells about your summertime experiences.

Creating the Glyph

1. Cut out the sandcastle. Glue it to the center of a horizontal sheet of construction paper.

2. Read and answer each question on the legend. Follow these directions to represent
your answers on the glyph:
- Question 1: Cut out the towers and glue one to each side of the sandcastle.
- Question 2: Color the sandcastle and towers.
- Question 3: Cut out the flag that corresponds to your answer. Glue it to the
top of one of the towers.
- Question 4: Glue the appropriate seashells near the bottom of the sandcastle.

3. Color the flag and seashells. If desired, glue a light layer of sand around the glyph as
well. Then write your name on the back of the glyph.

Extend Learning

Ask children to tell how the glyphs can be used to find out what treat is the class
favorite. Guide them to conclude that the shape of the seashells offers data about the
treats. First, create a three-column chart, labeling each heading with "Watermelon," "Ice
Pop," or "Lemonade." Then make a tick mark in the appropriate column for each glyph
that represents that kind of treat. Finally, help children count and compare the results to
determine the favorite treat.

TIP Use the glyph as a springboard to discuss
summer safety in the water and sun.

Math Skills

❈ geometry: shapes
❈ positional concepts
❈ counting

Materials

❈ glyph legend
and patterns
(pages 47–49)
❈ 12- by 18-inch
construction paper
❈ scissors
❈ glue
❈ crayons

Name _____

Summer Sandcastle
Legend

1 **Have you ever been to the beach?**

	yes	no
Type of Towers	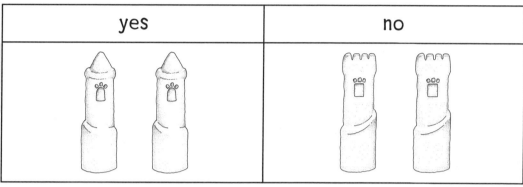	

2 **Have you ever built a sandcastle?**

	yes	no
Sandcastle Color	**yellow**	**light brown**

3 **What would you most enjoy doing at the beach?**

	build a sandcastle	swimming	collect seashells
Shape of Flag	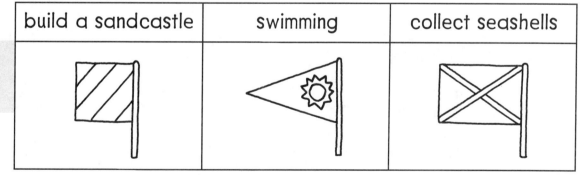		

4 **What summer treat would you most like to have on a hot day?**

	watermelon	ice pop	lemonade
Type of Seashells			

Just-Right Glyphs for Young Learners © 2010 by Pamela Chanko, Scholastic Teaching Resources

Summer Sandcastle
Castle, Flag, and Shell Patterns

Summer Sandcastle
Tower Patterns

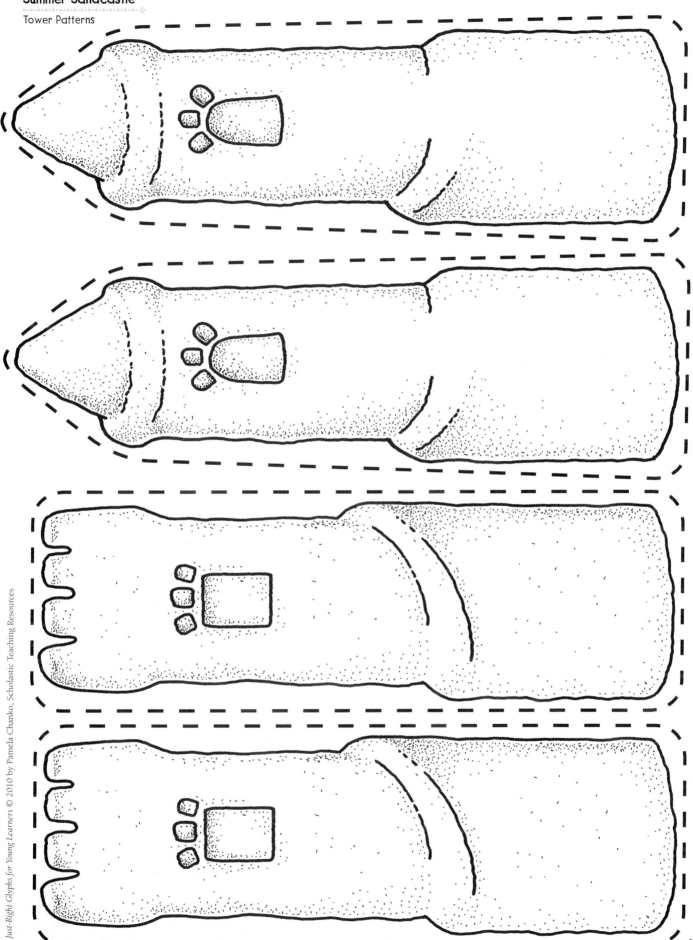

Let Freedom Ring

This Fourth of July glyph combines elements of two patriotic symbols:
the Liberty Bell and the Stars and Stripes! While creating the glyph, children have
the opportunity to share their preferences about the holiday and our country.

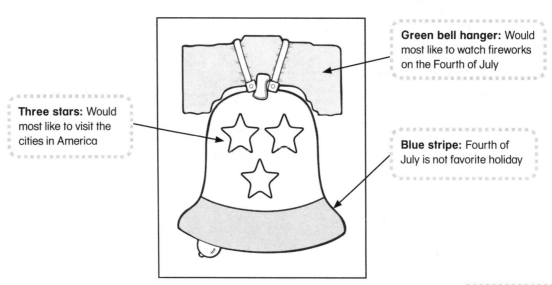

Green bell hanger: Would most like to watch fireworks on the Fourth of July

Three stars: Would most like to visit the cities in America

Blue stripe: Fourth of July is not favorite holiday

Getting Started

Create your own glyph and mark your responses on the legend. Then display your glyph and discuss it with children. Guide them to use the legend to determine what each feature on the glyph tells about you.

Creating the Glyph

1. Cut out the bell. Glue it to a vertical sheet of construction paper.

2. Read and answer each question on the legend. Follow these directions to represent your answers on the glyph:
   • Question 1: Color the stripe at the bottom of the bell.
   • Question 2: Color the bell hanger.
   • Question 3: Cut out the number of stars that corresponds to your answer. Glue them to the bell above the stripe.

3. Color the bell and stars, if desired. Also, to add sparkle to the bell, glue on glitter that matches the stars and stripe. Then write your name on the back of the glyph.

Extend Learning

Challenge children to put the glyphs in order according to the color of the bell hanger: gray, brown, or green. Then ask them to tell what each group of glyphs has in common. (Each represents a different preference of how to celebrate the holiday.) Use this as a springboard to discuss other ways people might celebrate, such as having a barbeque, going to a concert, and playing sports.

Math Skills

❋ geometry: shapes
❋ positional concepts
❋ counting

Materials

❋ glyph legend and patterns (pages 51–52)
❋ 9- by 12-inch construction paper
❋ scissors
❋ glue
❋ red and blue crayons

Name _____

Let Freedom Ring
Legend

1 Is the Fourth of July your favorite holiday?

yes	no
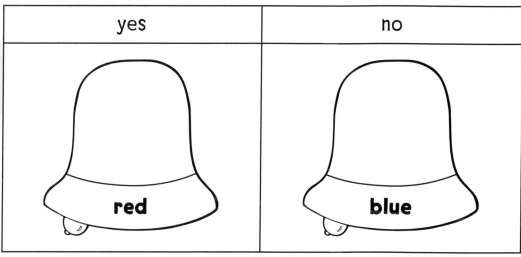	

Stripe Color on Bell

red | blue

2 How would you most like to celebrate the Fourth of July?

have a picnic	go to a parade	watch fireworks
gray	**brown**	**green**

Color of Bell Hanger

3 What parts of America would you most like to visit?

the deserts	the forests	the cities	something else

Number of Stars on Bell

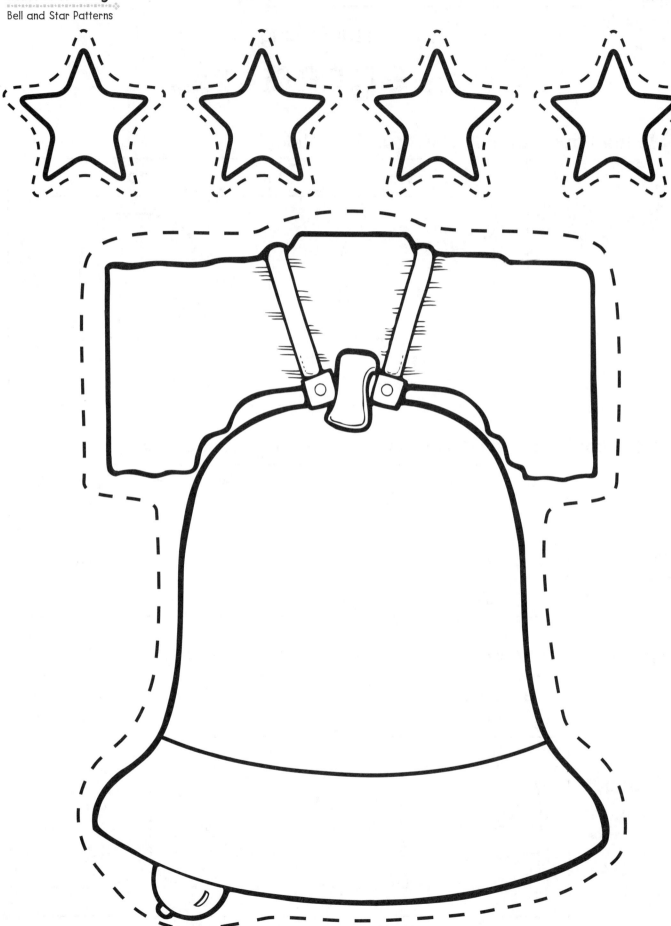

Just-Right Glyphs for Young Learners © 2010 by Pamela Chanko, Scholastic Teaching Resources

All-About-Me Hat

A snazzy hat can say a lot about a person—and this hat tells some very important information!
Use this glyph as a getting-to-know-you or anytime activity to review basic class statistics,
such as the number of girls and boys, as well as individual information about each child.

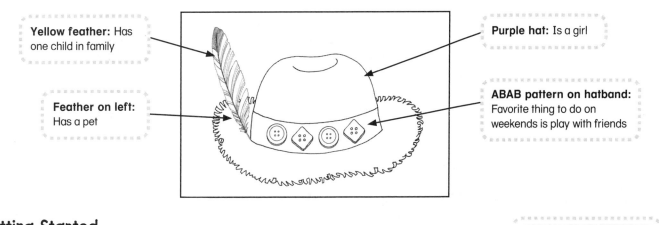

Yellow feather: Has one child in family

Feather on left: Has a pet

Purple hat: Is a girl

ABAB pattern on hatband: Favorite thing to do on weekends is play with friends

Getting Started

Create your own glyph and mark your responses on the legend. Then display your glyph and discuss it with children. Guide them to use the legend to determine what each feature on the glyph tells about you.

Creating the Glyph

1. Cut out the hat. Glue it to a horizontal sheet of construction paper.

2. Read and answer each question on the legend. Follow these directions to represent your answers on the glyph:
  - Question 1: Color the hat.
  - Question 2: Cut out the button pattern that goes with your answer. Glue it to the hatband.
  - Question 3: Cut out and color the feather according to your answer.
  - Question 4: Glue the feather to the side of the hat based on your answer.

3. Color the hatband and buttons. Write your name on the back of the glyph.

Extend Learning

Ask children: *What weekend activity is the girls' favorite?* Then help them sort the glyphs into two groups: boys and girls. Next, have them sort the "Girls" glyphs by the button pattern on the hatbands, count how many glyphs feature each pattern, and compare the numbers to determine which pattern appears on the most glyphs. What activity does this represent? Explain that this is the favorite weekend activity of most girls. Repeat, using the "Boys" glyphs to find the boys' favorite weekend activity.

Math Skills

- ✳ geometry: shapes
- ✳ patterns
- ✳ positional concepts
- ✳ counting

Materials

- ✳ glyph legend and patterns (pages 54–56)
- ✳ 12- by 18-inch construction paper
- ✳ scissors
- ✳ glue
- ✳ crayons

TIP Invite children to interpret their glyphs to the class, providing additional information about themselves as they share.

Name _____

All-About-Me Hat

 Legend

1 **Are you a girl or a boy?**

	girl	boy
Color of Hat	**purple**	**red**

2 **What is your favorite thing to do on weekends?**

	play with friends	watch TV	read books	something else
Button Pattern on Hatband	⦿◇⦿◇	⦿⦿◇◇	◇⦿⦿◇	⦿◇◇⦿

3 **How many children are in your family?**

	one child	two children	three children	four or more children
Color of Feather	**yellow**	**orange**	**green**	**blue**

4 **Do you have a pet?**

	yes	no
Position of Feather on Hat	**left side**	**right side**

Just-Right Glyphs for Young Learners © 2010 by Pamela Chanko, Scholastic Teaching Resources

All-About-Me Hat
Hat Pattern

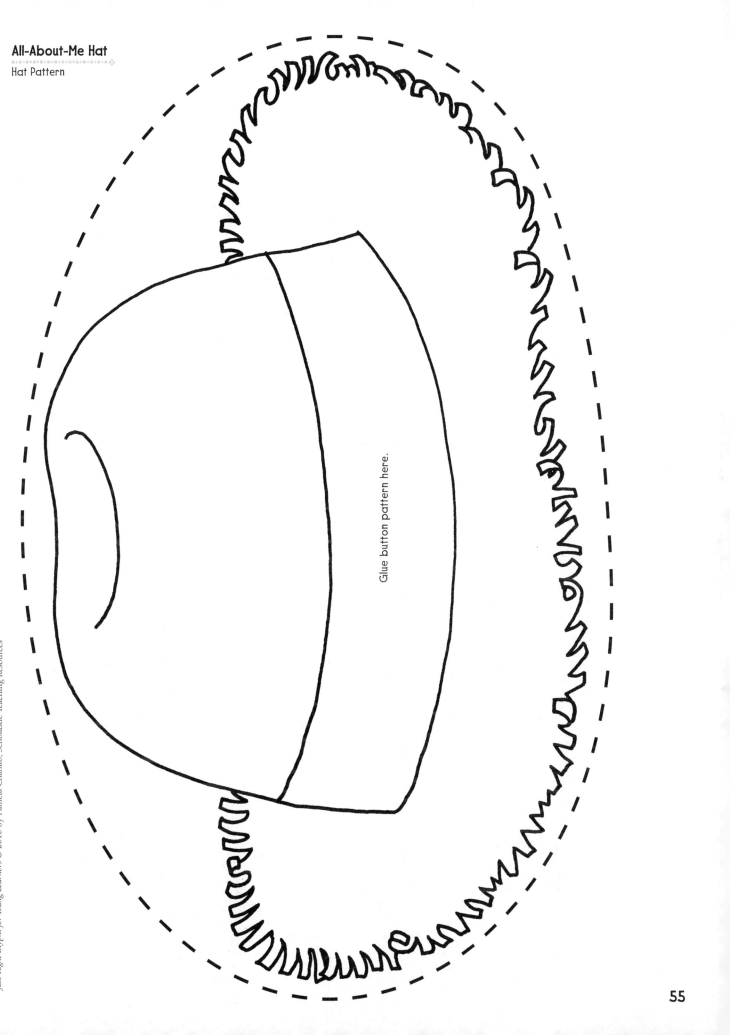

Glue button pattern here.

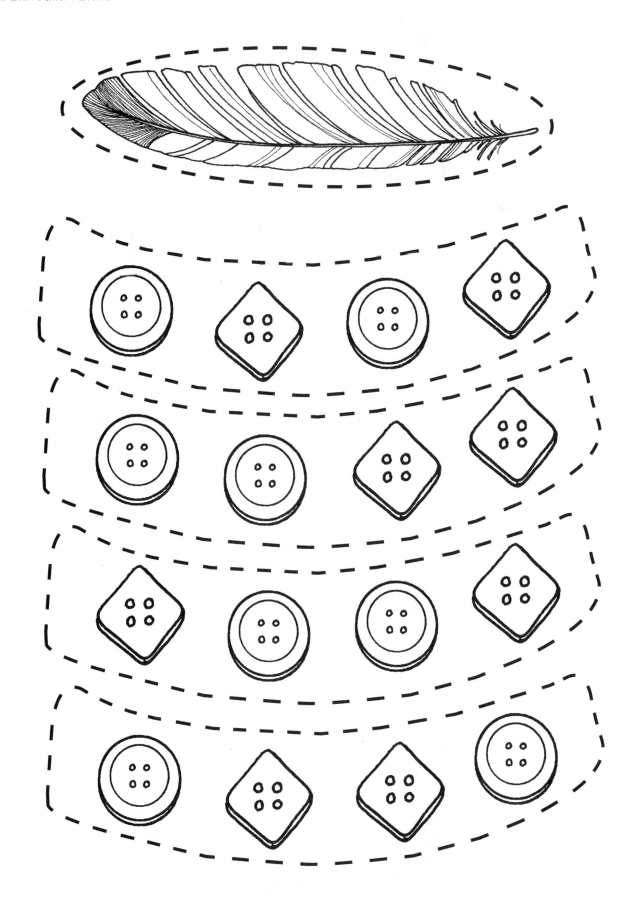

Just-Right Glyphs for Young Learners © 2010 by Pamela Chanko, Scholastic Teaching Resources

Birthday Wishes

Most children can't wait for their birthday to arrive.
This glyph gives them a way to tell a few things about their
special day—and to celebrate it any time!

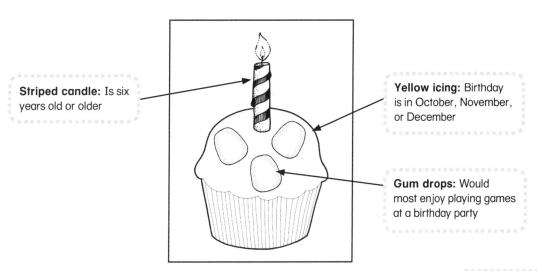

Striped candle: Is six years old or older

Yellow icing: Birthday is in October, November, or December

Gum drops: Would most enjoy playing games at a birthday party

Getting Started

Create your own glyph and mark your responses on the legend. Then display your glyph and discuss it with children. Guide them to use the legend to determine what each feature on the glyph tells about you.

Creating the Glyph

1. Cut out the cupcake. Glue it to a vertical sheet of construction paper.

2. Read and answer each question on the legend. Follow these directions to represent your answers on the glyph:
  - Question 1: Color the icing on the cupcake.
  - Question 2: Cut out the candle that corresponds to your answer. Glue it on the cupcake.
  - Question 3: Cut out the candy shapes that correspond to your answer. Glue them on the cupcake.

3. Color the cupcake wrapper, candle, and candies. Write your name on the back of the glyph.

Extend Learning

Use the glyphs to create a birthday timeline to display throughout the year! First, ask children to attach a sticky note with the month and day of their birthday to their glyph. Next, have them sort the glyphs by icing color (into 3-month groupings) and help them order each group of glyphs by month and then the day of the month on which each birthday occurs. Finally, have children sequence all of the glyphs, from January through December, along a horizontal line to create a timeline.

Math Skills

※ geometry: shapes
※ patterns
※ positional concepts
※ counting

Materials

※ glyph legend and patterns (pages 58–59)
※ 9- by 12-inch construction paper
※ scissors
※ glue
※ crayons

Name _____

Birthday Wishes
✥ Legend ✥

❶ In what month is your birthday?

	January, February, or March	April, May, or June	July, August, or September	October, November, or December
Color of Icing	light blue	pink	light green	yellow

❷ How old are you now?

	five years old or younger	six years old or older
Type of Candle		

❸ What would you most enjoy about a birthday party?

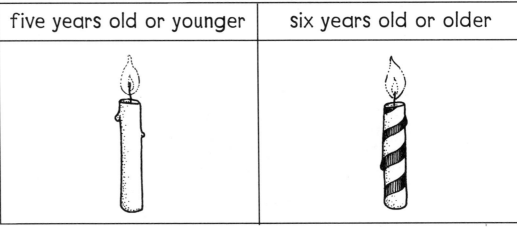

	singing "Happy Birthday"	playing games	eating birthday treats
Shape of Candy Toppings			

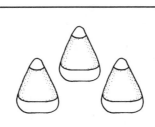  

Just-Right Glyphs for Young Learners © 2010 by Pamela Chanko, Scholastic Teaching Resources

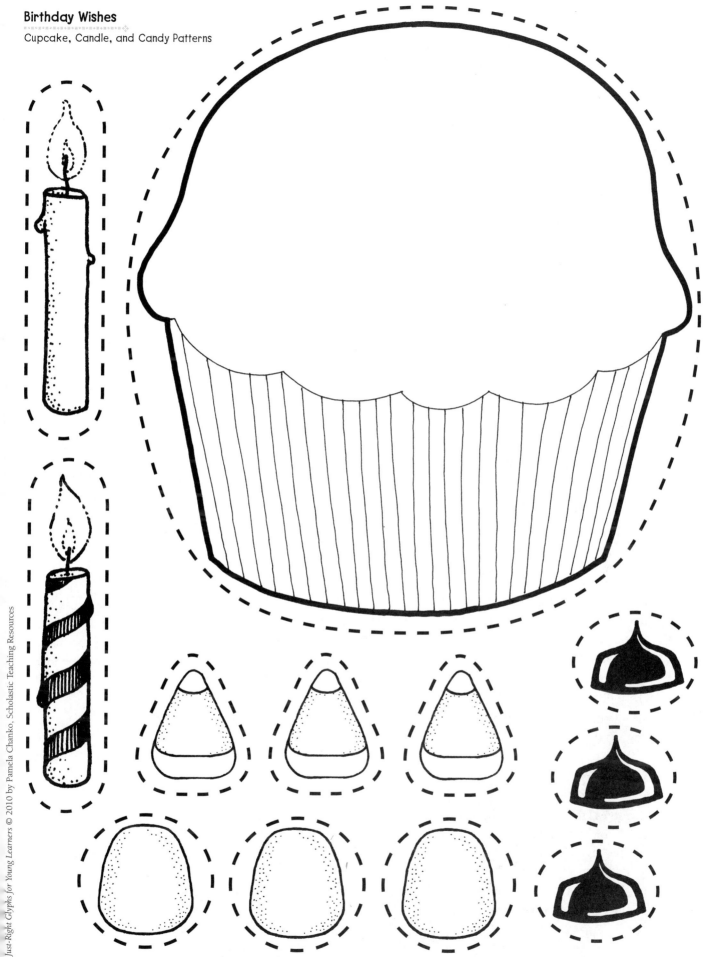

Birthday Wishes
Cupcake, Candle, and Candy Patterns

✼⟰ Use Your Noodle! ⟰✼

Mmm! What could be yummier than a bowl of noodles? With this glyph, children create their own dish filled with data that tells about their favorite food.

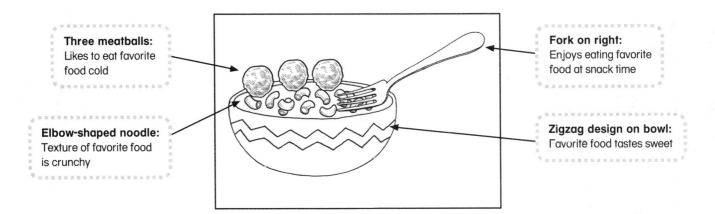

Three meatballs: Likes to eat favorite food cold

Elbow-shaped noodle: Texture of favorite food is crunchy

Fork on right: Enjoys eating favorite food at snack time

Zigzag design on bowl: Favorite food tastes sweet

Getting Started

Create your own glyph and mark your responses on the legend. Then display your glyph and discuss it with children. Guide them to use the legend to determine what each feature on the glyph tells about your favorite food.

Creating the Glyph

1. Cut out the bowl. Glue it to a horizontal sheet of construction paper.

2. Read and answer each question on the legend. Follow these directions to represent your answers on the glyph:

- Questions 1–2: Cut out the patterns with the bowl design and type of noodles that correspond to each answer. Glue each piece to the bowl.
- Question 3: Cut out the number of meatballs that corresponds to your answer. Glue them on top of (but not covering) the noodles.
- Question 4: Cut out the fork. Glue it to the side of the bowl that corresponds to your answer.

3. Color the glyph. (Avoid covering up any designs or patterns that show data.) Write your name on the back of the glyph.

Extend Learning

Attach sticky notes labeled with children's names to their glyphs. Display the glyphs for a game of "I Spy" and secretly choose one for children to identify. Give one clue at a time about that glyph, for instance: *I spy a glyph that represents a salty food. The food is also crunchy. It is eaten hot. The person who made the glyph eats the food at mealtime. That person's name begins with V.* After children guess the correct glyph, they might also try to guess the glyph-maker's favorite food.

Math Skills

* patterns
* counting
* positional concepts

Materials

* glyph legend and patterns (pages 61–64)
* 12- by 18-inch construction paper
* scissors
* glue
* crayons

Name _____

Use Your Noodle!

✵⚬⚭ Legend ⚭⚬✵

1 **How does your favorite food taste?**

	sweet	salty	sour	another taste
Design on Bowl				

2 **What is the texture of your favorite food?**

	crunchy	soft	another texture
Type of Noodle			

3 **How do you most like to eat your favorite food?**

	warm	cold	at room temperature
Number of Meatballs			

4 **When do you most enjoy eating your favorite food?**

	at meal time	at snack time
Position of Fork to Bowl	**left**	**right**

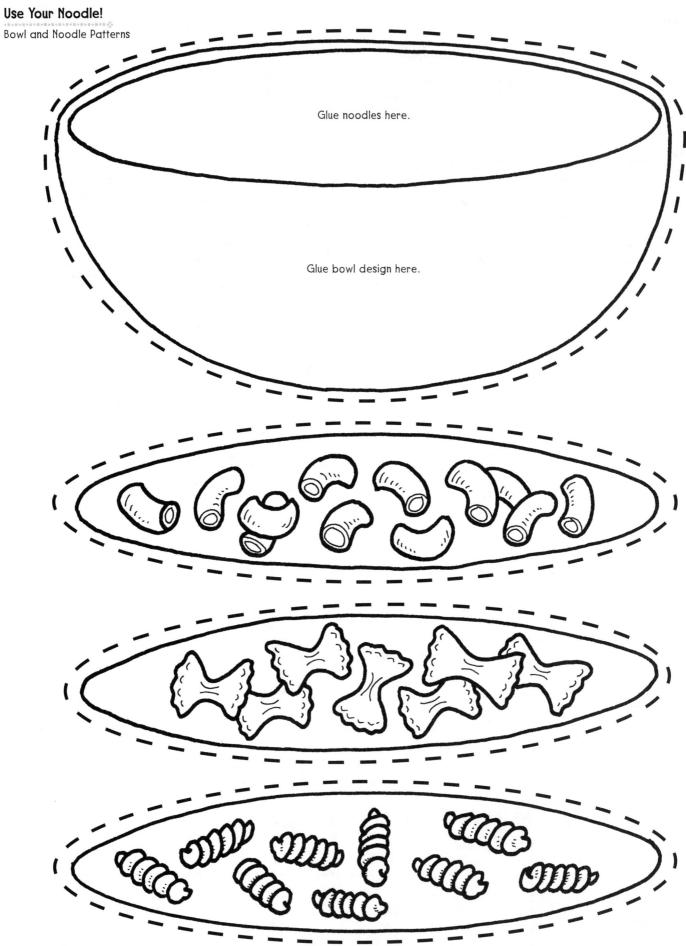

Glue noodles here.

Glue bowl design here.

Just-Right Glyphs for Young Learners © 2010 by Pamela Chanko, Scholastic Teaching Resources

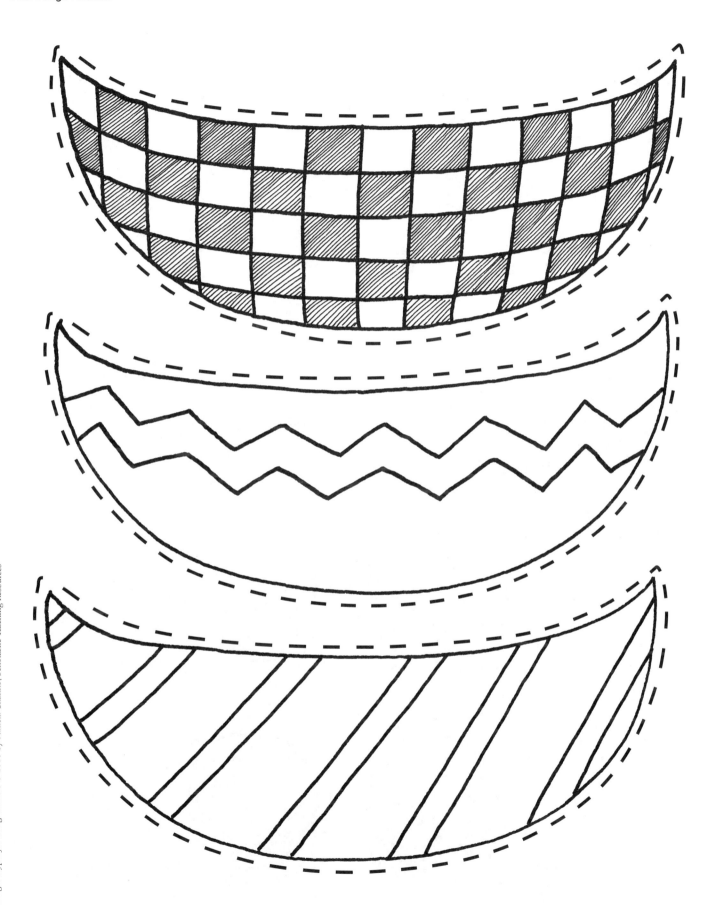

Use Your Noodle!

Bowl Design, Meatball, and Fork Patterns

Just-Right Glyphs for Young Learners © 2010 by Pamela Chanko, Scholastic Teaching Resources